T0197245

If the
WORLD
Didn't
SUCK
We'd All
FALL
OFF

If the WORLD Didn't SUCK We'd All FALL OFF

NICHOLAS THOMAS

IF THE WORLD DIDN'T SUCK WE'D ALL FALL OFF

iUniverse books may be ordered through booksellers or by contacting:

iUniverse
1663 Liberty Drive
Bloomington, IN 47403
www.iuniverse.com
1-800-Authors (1-800-288-4677)

ISBN: 978-1-5320-5207-1 (sc)
ISBN: 978-1-5320-5206-4 (e)

Library of Congress Control Number: 2018906941

Print information available on the last page.

iUniverse rev. date: 07/24/2018

Contents

PERSONAL

It was hard to write this poem,

To search my mind,

'Cause I was scared of what I might find.

The hate and pain that hides beneath,

Brings a tear with gritting teeth.

My life is so messed up now.

If I wanted to change I wouldn't know how.

I push harder every day,

To prove wrong what people say.

I skate, I hate, I love, I cry,

People just judge and pass me by.

I love and care for people that call me friend,

But are they really there until the end?

All these questions come from within,

Hurting me over again and again.

So if anyone has the answers,

And is not lying,

Please help for inside I am crying.

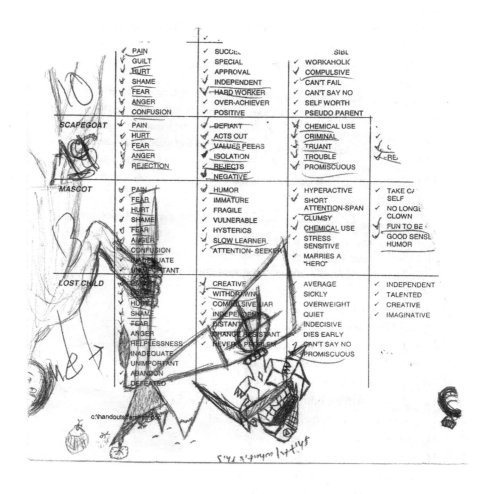

	PAIN	SUCCESS	WORKAHOLIC	SIBL...
	GUILT	SPECIAL	COMPULSIVE	
	HURT	APPROVAL	CAN'T FAIL	
	SHAME	INDEPENDENT	CAN'T SAY NO	
	FEAR	HARD WORKER	SELF WORTH	
	ANGER	OVER-ACHIEVER	PSEUDO PARENT	
	CONFUSION	POSITIVE		
SCAPEGOAT	PAIN	DEFIANT	CHEMICAL USE	
	HURT	ACTS OUT	CRIMINAL	
	FEAR	VALUES PEERS	TRUANT	RE...
	ANGER	ISOLATION	TROUBLE	
	REJECTION	REJECTS	PROMISCUOUS	
		NEGATIVE		
MASCOT	PAIN	HUMOR	HYPERACTIVE	TAKE CARE SELF
	FEAR	IMMATURE	SHORT ATTENTION-SPAN	NO LONGER CLOWN
	HURT	FRAGILE	CLUMSY	FUN TO BE
	SHAME	VULNERABLE	CHEMICAL USE	GOOD SENSE HUMOR
	FEAR	HYSTERICS	STRESS SENSITIVE	
	ANGER	SLOW LEARNER	MARRIES A "HERO"	
	CONFUSION	ATTENTION-SEEKER		
	INADEQUATE			
	UNIMPORTANT			
LOST CHILD	PAIN	CREATIVE	AVERAGE	INDEPENDENT
	GUILT	WITHDRAWN	SICKLY	TALENTED
	HURT	COMPULSIVE LIAR	OVERWEIGHT	CREATIVE
	SHAME	INDEPENDENT	QUIET	IMAGINATIVE
	FEAR	DISTANT	INDECISIVE	
	ANGER	CHANGE RESISTANT	DIES EARLY	
	HELPLESSNESS	NEVER A PROBLEM	CAN'T SAY NO	
	INADEQUATE		PROMISCUOUS	
	UNIMPORTANT			
	ABANDON			
	DEFEATED			

c:\handouts\...doc

Depressed and down with a frown,
Lost in despair without a care,
When she's not there.
Missing those beautiful, blue green eyes and reddish-blond hair.
My little girl is everything I love,
I wish every day I could give her a kiss and huge hug.
Everyday away brings dismay,
It hurts so very much,
Not to hear her voice or feel her touch.
No matter whatever you do or where ever you go,
Adamaya I love you and miss you so.
Depressed and down with a frown,
Lost in despair without a care,
When she's not there.
Into my heart the emotions tear.
Not the muscle one that pumps the blood,
The heart that produces love like some unknown drug,
For my child.
Producing parental instincts, ferocious and wild.
For her I'd fight everything, all in all.
I'd fight the seasons such as the fall, I'd fight the leaves and the trees,
I'd fight the leaves that fall off the trees.
I'd fight the air humanity breathes.
I'd fight the earth and the sun, the universe and beyond.
I know everyone with their own Adamaya knows,
Where their child's name goes.
Locked away deep in the heart, so it can never depart.
These words are for you kiddo,
So you know what I would do and how far I'd go.
Publish it to the whole world, just to show,
When you're not around, my emotional state is down,
On my face I wear this frown.
I love you Adamaya, until and after they put me into the ground.

I'm tired of hurting everyone around me,

Without moving a muscle or making a peep.

I chose not to speak,

I chose not to grieve,

I chose not to believe in them and how they deceive.

To all the pain felt by others,

I'm sorry to be me.

I'm sorry I'll never meet every need,

I'm sorry you'll never hear me leave.

I've been broken long before,

I've been out spoken in the wrong war.

I've been so hurt and know how it feels,

I apologize for real, from me to you and your ordeals.

I've experienced more than I hope any of you,

Ever have to endure.

I'm sorry to thee from me, Nick T.

METAPHORIC

Mind boggled in a heap,

Can't sleep, life's waters are getting deep.

This confining place is driving me insane,

Tearing me apart, hurting my brain.

Looking out this slit,

Only see it,

One star in the sky,

Sometimes I just wish I could die.

My life's one big messed up lie,

No room to be down, no room to cry.

Never getting better, always getting worse,

Sometimes I just feel like I'm under a curse.

Mind boggled in a heap,

Can't sleep, life's waters are getting deep.

I need a life jacket,

But my life's so messed up, no one else can hack it.

I have no one to throw me a rope,

My family's crazy and my friends are all on dope.

Well screw it; I guess I'll just drown.

I'm tired of this craziness anyway, I'm sick of messing around.

Mind boggled in a heap, can't sleep,

Life's waters are getting deep.

Running like a wild fire, across the plains,
Coming quick, engulfing you in flames.
Followed by silence, calming the violence,
Shake your head, you're not dead.
More alive than ever, lighter than a feather,
Let the animal out of the cage, burn off some rage.
Get a taste of blood, while rolling in the mud,
Usually only white but a little red will be alright.
The mist is in the air, stripping everything bare,
Watching the scenery deteriorate, not falling for the bait.
13 miles ahead, is what the wise man said,
Snatching up the scroll, getting ready to roll.
Riding the white line, sun in your eyes, making you blind,
Heading for the hills, fish like gills.
Riding the coaster, with green and white,
Better watch out, there's gonna be a fight.
Beat each other down, as the ride goes round,
Beginning to slow, energy getting low.
Time for the feast, have to feed the beast,
Back in the cage, beginning to feel the rage.
Running wild like a fire, across the plains,
Coming quick, engulfing you in flames.

Life is colorful, upside down,
Not ever wanting to touch the ground.
It's hard when that's all you know,
Nowhere else to turn, no place to go.
The colors are always a friend,
Never leaving in the end.
They twist and turn; it's hard to see,
What life without the colors could be?
I love the colors, they make me happy,
Green and purple and laffy taffy.
Oh, that is not a color, it is a candy,
But eating one will make you dandy.
All of them are so good,
If I could have more, I would.
Life if colorful upside down,
Not ever wanting to touch the ground.

Fo sho.
You know what it's fo,
You turn the handle, to open the do.
Ahead but behind, stuck in fast forward,
Waiting to rewind, rock the fuck out.
Slow it and see what it's all about,
We all go around, to keep from falling down.
Memories in a pile, memories in a file,
Make paper airplanes and burn them in style.
Erase the bad taste and get back to the race,
Can't feel my face.
Time to clean it up, before you fill the cup,
How's it dirty but clean is what you seen?
You know the deal, do what you feel,
And always keep it real.

The Sky Will Cry

I watch the rain fall,

Waiting for a call.

I wonder if I'll make it through another cloudy sky,

And when it comes how will I die.

I ponder all of life's choices,

But it's interrupted by angry voices.

I try to not be so strange,

Then I look at myself,

And see nothing to change.

The sky will cry as the day passes by,

Then it will clear,

And night will be here.

In my cell, I dwell on these,
Problems as they swell.
Who do I tell and what do I say?
Dismay is life, no hope for me and them and they.
No point to continue,
No readable menu,
No past, no future,
Is what I remember of her.
No time, no minutes,
No truth, only gimmicks.
In my cell, I dwell as,
It all begins to swell.
Engulfing me in its agony,
Goodbye, I'm gone, no more Nick T.
For you all to see,
Swallowed up by this sea,
Of problems surrounding me.

✳

DIRECTIONAL

Strange people, strange places,

New decisions, new faces.

Never ending days, dark rooms,

Filled with haze.

Smoke something nice,

Roll another dice.

Everyone lives in fear,

Asking over and over, why are we here?

There is no point,

Roll another joint.

Pass it to a friend,

Waiting for the end.

Will it come soon?

After another moon?

Pushing through the days,

Trying to clear the haze.

Another day passes by,

Trying so hard to catch that high.

Twisted in Two

Twisted inside, on a crazy ride.

Tearing me in two, not knowing what to do.

Fading to black, fading to white,

Not knowing, whether to turn back or to fight.

It's hurting my head, while lying in bed,

Feeling the burning, tossing and turning.

This crazy ride has twisted me inside.

Tearing me in two,

Stuck, not knowing what to do.

No Wires to Harness

Tired, unwired,

Wireless no wires to harness.

No motivations, to keep chasing, racing,

Climbing up that ladder.

Why should I care, when it has no matter?

How can I possibly get any sadder?

Madder, hurt, burnt,

I needed you there and you weren't.

From that, a lot I learnt.

Learning, burning, building, yielding,

Perfection comes with much complexion.

Complication, dedication, no inflation in my life.

No way to envision that these decisions,

Will take me to what's right.

So I write, I fight, I creep and never sleep in the night.

What did I do, to anyone, to be done,

So wrong? Been beat down for so long.

Their hating makes me hate them,

Them haters with so much hatred.

Hate for this redhead, this Redman,

I'm talking about me. Don't you understand?

✶

LIFE

Stare at the screen,

Feel my mind fiend.

Not sure for what,

Am I just a slut?

Take your turn,

Leave another burn.

I'm just a lost soul,

Glass half empty, never half full.

Sitting in the dark,

See a little spark,

Light a fire in my heart.

A little water and paper falls apart.

Try to draw another one,

But it's too late, the damage is already done.

Pieces of me float in the waves,

Can't find my way through this maze.

Stare a little more,

Open another door.

Feel a little hate,

Can't think straight.

I'm just a lost soul,

Glass half empty, never half full.

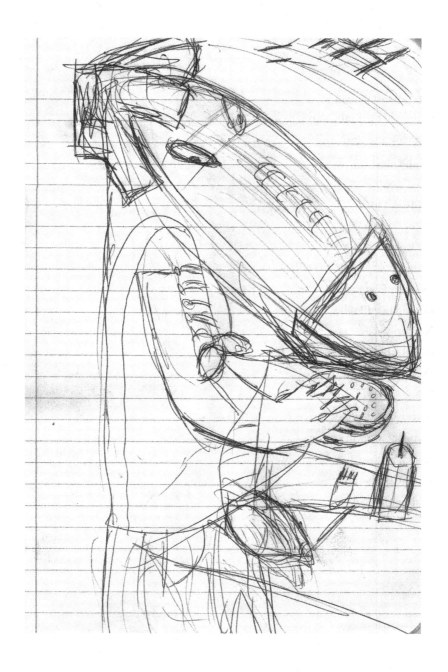

31

A room full of people,

Only two I actually know.

Who are the rest?

Is it for the best?

I'm not sure,

It's all a blur.

What do I do?

Do I put on a mask?

Be nice, pass around the flask,

Everyone's going fast.

How long will it last?

Not for sure,

It's all a blur.

Draw on the wall.

Who's going to call?

A knock at the door,

Someone wanting more.

Just go away.

Fade with the sun,

Ending the day.

Unclear Intentions

Tension wrenchin, tense from unclear intentions.

My attention is intended for a higher intellect,

I'm indifferent in my opinion, so different then these imprisoned.

Society slaves, over paid maids, to which we throw parades,

And give their own days.

I say what the fuck, then switch it up,

And scream; fuck the world, everyone except my little girl.

She is the pearl, in my life of dirt,

Love her so much, my heart it hurt.

I'm unstable in this life of mine, that's not mine.

Owned by them, swept under the table, under the rug,

Swept away, under the influence of this drug.

Slept not at all, this day or 8,

Don't know anything but dismay for my life's fate.

Tense from unclear intentions,

Here I sit tension wrenchin.

34

Beating me down again and again,

With all your lies, a piece of my heart dies.

Don't care of the cost,

Years of trust lost,

Not even knowing, how I keep going.

How can I make it another day?

Is there anyway?

I ask why?

But it doesn't matter if I cry.

I close my eyes,

With all your lies, a piece of my heart dies.

Beating me down again and again,

How long can I fight if there's no way to win?

Beaten so much, feel no touch,

Numb to the world.

With all your lies, a piece of my heart dies,

How much can you fake? How much will you take?

? LIFE

Broken pieces in the creases.

Am I supposed to do, what I do? And if so,

For who?

Is it destiny, already planned for me?

Is it a story already told? And,

If so, why can't I see how it will unfold?

Load the boat, hope it will float,

Hit the sea, not being able to see.

What is out there?

Something in the way, it's not fair.

Have to go around or travel over ground,

Never hearing the put downs,

Life's full of smiles and frowns.

It's on each knee, spilt apart, unsure which to be,

Both at the same time.

Hear the wind chime,

I see them lookin, wondering what I might be cookin.

Nothing you can eat! Something to sweep you off your feet.

Gone as fast as it came, never living life the same.

Get a little lazy, maybe a little crazy,

Freak out, scream and shout.

Be calm,

Offer out your palm,

Take their arm, lead them away,

To return another day.

Broken pieces in the creases.

Am I supposed to do, what I do and if so,

For who?

Roll another,

Smoke another.

Thoughts astir,

Life's a blur.

Ride the jet stream,

What does it all mean?

Just an animal trapped,

In life's cage,

Enraged, at the fullest stage.

Thoughts astir,

Life's a blur.

Can't see straight,

Everyone has the same fate.

Darkness, the night will bring,

Love and hate everything.

Thoughts astir,

Life's a blur.

Just a jet stream,

What does it all mean?

Roll another,

Smoke another.

So lost in life, here this night,
In the sky twinkles a light.
No wish granted, must not be enchanted,
But you know I've been branded.
By life's many scars like nights many stars,
And prisons many unbendable bars.
Why is what I've always asked,
Why is what I still have never grasped.
Nothing in my hands, nothing upon these lands,
No one in my grandstands, except emptiness.
A canvas unmarked, a body so scarred.
When I close these eyes, I see my fate,
Darkness everywhere and no heavenly gate.
Is it true, are all the actions matter less that we do?
A performance with no audience,
Grandstands where not a single person stands,
No clapping hands or cheering fans.
So lost I am in life,
Tonight under this starry sky.

Life's a war, that's for shore.

Cops always at the door.

Staring at the ceiling, while lying on the floor.

Another dark night in a situation,

That's just not right.

Right on the edge, looking for the feds,

Life moves fast looking at the past.

Stay ahead of the game,

While trying to stay sane.

Will the road come to an end?

Maybe around the next bend?

Another night, another fight,

A little ganja and it'll be alright.

This bumpy road is hard to drive,

Fighting unendingly to stay alive.

Everything's crazy, I don't know what to think,

Everything changes in the fraction of a blink.

Life's messed up, unpredictable and corrupt,

It's a war, that's for shore.

Staring at the ceiling, while lying on the floor.

2,000
850 Rent 2 months March, April
1,150 MAY BDAY 24 years

Unanswered Whys

Sitting on the bed, pondering thoughts in my head.

Peak out the slit, can't see shit.

Open your eyes, life's full of lies,

Big fat question marks with unanswered whys.

No one knows for real, if you go to hell if you steal,

Or follow a bright light, if you please your god just right.

Just a question mark, with no spark in the dark.

Choices have to be made; the game of life has to be played.

What decisions do I make? What direction do I take?

Can't think straight.

Has someone already decided my fate?

Peak out the slit, still can't see shit.

What is it that I'm looking for?

A paved road or open door?

It's hard to believe how fast life goes,

And scary to think where it actually flows.

Open your eyes, life's full of lies,

Big fast question marks,

And unanswered whys.

I look at life different than most,

Maybe in a brighter light or on a higher post.

I don't understand,

Why no one's there to give me a hand.

I sit here and let my mind stir,

For what reason I'm not really sure.

There ain't shit to see, just the same old bullshit, the same old me.

This life is out of control, spiraling and spiraling down the hole.

Am I here alone; is there no one at the other end of the phone?

Why do I feel this way, why do I feel like I try so hard every day?

Am I a ghost among the most or am I just a brain,

Expanding and expanding while the earth feels the strain.

Are we just a mass put here to see how long we last?

Are all you people in denial? Every Sunday in by the millions you file,

To take your chairs and hope some god will hear your prayers.

It's all just a fairytale to keep everyone behind the veil,

You don't actually know, so you look to where you can't go.

There's no one there, no one to take your hand, no one to love and care.

No one's up there picking and choosing we're all fucked everyone,

Ends up losing.

PAIN

I'm trapped and broken,

Friends fade with words unspoken.

People change and become strange,

Those you thought you could trust,

Leave you coughing in the dust.

Where do you turn? Where do you go?

Who will be there 'til the end?

And how will you really know?

Never can, never will, not worth the trouble,

So burn in hell.

What the heck? Why the heck? How the heck?

Could you be so blind, so ignorant?

Give you something straight and it comes back bent.

I hate you; I hate your personality,

I hate that you can't see reality.

Open your eyes, let the blinds rise,

Take in some fresh air, as much as you can bare.

Smoke some rezz, hit the road,

Global travel, no more gravel travel.

Expand the mind,

Look for what you can't find.

AND
PEOPLE
HATE
ME
THE
QUESTION
IS IS
THAT
ALWAYS
HOW
IT'S
GOING
TO
BE

There is no love any more it feels
like someone slam the door I
wish I knew what love was supost
to mean it can do frrked up shit and
turn you into a demon & you'll have
a frrked up feeling maybe its not even
worth the reality so fuck I give up

If this is how hate is ment to be, to piss the world off and turn
every one aglanst me. I guess that's what a person gets that's full of
negativity, maybe this is not only the person I want to be and have
people see me

49

Driven Insane

What a mess, all this stress,

All this pain, driving me insane.

Life's going downhill,

Down and down, it just won't stay still.

I miss the ones I love, I miss my girls.

Watching Adamaya play, brightens up the darkest day.

A soft touch from my sexy momma,

Blocks out all the bullshit, hate and drama.

But that is no more,

I messed up and she walked out the door.

Taking my soul, turning my heart as black and dead as coal.

I push as hard as I can,

But it's crushing; it's killing me with its powerful hand.

What a mess, all this stress,

All this pain has driven me insane.

※

LOSS

Someone Close Becomes a Ghost

Life fades away in the blink of an eye,

And you're stuck just wondering why.

Why did they have to die?

Leaving us all behind to cry.

Watching another one go,

Brings out those feelings we try not to show.

Now we are without another,

Friend, mother, father, sister or brother.

Someone close becomes a ghost.

It sucks when that person we loved has to leave,

And we can't do anything but think and grieve.

All we can do is stick together and look out for one another.

Be there 'til the end,

Like a true friend.

This wicked riddle,

Spits like a boiling tea kettle.

She loves me not, said every last rose petal.

Time kills,

Poppin pills,

Government seals,

Struggling to provide his kids meals.

So he steals, then himself he kills and the reason he never,

Reveals.

Why cry out to everybody?

If you had no words for anybody,

Not even me, what did I do?

I was the one that understood and could.

I always cared for you.

Still do, to this very day and every day.

I cry inside, goodbye,

All I wanna know is why?

What was so bad you had to die?

When I asked if you're okay, why did you have to lie?

Inside I still cry, goodbye, farewell.

If you're as bad as they say, I'll see you in hell.

'Cause I'm on the way real fast,

Backwards in reality, blast forward into the past.

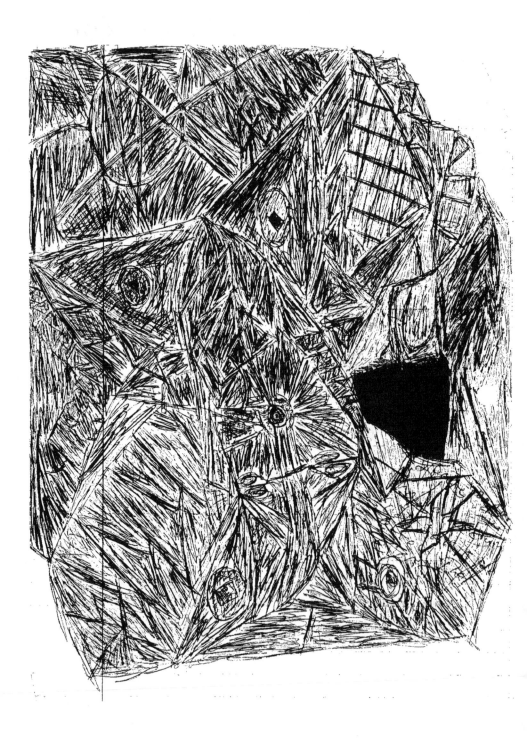

Another one bites the dust,

They say.

I trust they weren't experiencing the,

Pain we felt today or they wouldn't say it that way.

Another one we put into the dirt,

Everyone around you see is so hurt.

Tears streak cheeks for weeks,

So weak we grieve, can't think.

One blink life's over.

Who would have thought the flow would go,

So fast, times have changed and things never last.

But we're together,

From past to present, to the future and forever.

Stand together, love each other,

Only one life not another.

After which we hope to hover,

Above the world and be angels helping,

The ones we love, forever more above they sore.

Another one bites the dust,

They say, I trust they didn't experience the pain we felt,

Today or they wouldn't say it that way.

End of the Show

Where did life go?

It's gone, it's over,

That's the end of the show.

Please exit to the left, fast not slow.

Here's death and a hole,

Down you lay and in you'll go.

That's all there is to it,

No point to pursue it.

I'm angry and hateful,

And angrily unfaithful.

I don't get it,

It's bullshit.

Why do we get life?

If we can't keep it?

Another gone upon this dawn,

Another to rest as the moon will crest.

Soon I'll join you like the rest,

Goodbye, farewell, I'll see you in hell.

HOPE

Another word, still unheard,

Lost in my mind, searching and searching,

But nothing to find.

Open the gate to my fate, no silver plate,

Harsh and bitter masks full of eyeliner and glitter.

Fight back, scream and attack.

It's my life; you have no right to control the knife!

Fight back, scream and attack, take the knife, control your own life.

It's only write cause it's not right.

Full of light, way too bright.

Scream and attack, must fight back!

Stand your ground without a sound,

Let it all out, don't forget to scout.

Still unheard, another lost word,

Nothing to find, searching and searching, lost in my mind.

People see me as someone I'm not,

Turn their backs and let the friendships rot.

It's painful to think that way,

But it's proven by what they do and say.

I try to say it's not true,

But it's there, it's what people do.

You can see it in their eyes and hear it in their lies.

I can read them like a book; see them like a movie,

All you want to do is beat me down, put a mask over me.

I will never fall, I'll keep standing tall.

You can't hurt my feelings, you can't get me behind.

You'll never destroy my mind.

It keeps on fighting, keeps on sighting,

The fakes before they're here.

So I'm already ready,

I have no fear.

Hang my Coat

Today comes with a sense of hope,
My family's all here as I hang my coat.
Been down in the dumps a real long time,
But fate seems to be playing my song.
When the wind hits the metal and begins to chime,
I've lived a life full of dismay and tons of crime.
But I'm taking it back, making it mine.
Got my feet on the ground as the earth goes round,
Everyone's beginning to hear my sound.
The doors have opened as I stand here hoping,
They stay that way, day thru day.
Down on my knees, I begin to pray,
To anyone listening or looking my way.
They must be seeing and hearing my cry,
Blessing me by keeping Adamaya by my side.
They must know that she's my world,
Cause I couldn't make it thru life without my little girl.
Blessed thee who sees me down on my knees,
Please, oh please, keep me and my family free of disease.
And everyone else breathing oxygen,
From these trees.
Today comes with a sense of hope,
My family's all here as I hang my coat.
I see all these people looking up to me,
Been down a long time now I'm back on my feet.
I'm gonna keep on walkin, keep on trottin,
Thru this life without my knife.
Don't need that shit got my family.

We hip to hip, hand in hand,

When I got my family up in my clan.

Don't need no fans up in the grandstands,

With their clappin hands.

You know today comes with a sense of hope,

When my family's all here as I hang my coat.

And if you want to know the truth,

I love all of you.

If I didn't have you, I wouldn't know what to do.

So hear the words,

All my nouns and verbs.

If my parents didn't teach me to drive I'd,

Be rampin the curbs.

Christa and Trav, if you weren't in my life,

Who the hell would I have had to fight?

Trav's man and Christa's girl too, I love you.

Just the same as they do, well minus a couple things,

Few but your always in my heart and part of my crew.

And Kelsey, I know you're not wealthy and a little bit,

Stealthy but I love you babe, in love I'm your slave.

This ain't no game 'cause I don't play around when it comes,

To love, you know I'm the fiend and you're my drug.

Of course, I save the best for last, Adamaya,

You're up above the A class, my course you passed,

When it comes to my love for you, no mass can grasp,

Consuming everything in its path.

Now everyone knows I have this hope,

When my family's all here as I hang my coat.

Printed in the United States
By Bookmasters